The Preparation of the Gospel

DAG HEWARD-MILLS

Parchment House

Unless otherwise stated, all Scripture quotations are taken from the King James Version of the Bible.

THE PREPARATION OF THE GOSPEL

Find out more about Dag Heward-Mills
Healing Jesus Campaign
Write to: evangelist@daghewardmills.org
Website: www.daghewardmills.org
Facebook: Dag Heward-Mills
Twitter: @EvangelistDag

ISBN: 978-1-64330-522-6

Contents

1. The Art of Preparation 1

2. To Prepare is to Rehearse Ahead of Time........................ 7

3. To Prepare is to Foresee Problems................................. 17

4. To Prepare is to Educate Yourself with Special
   Knowledge.. 21

5. To Prepare is to Mellow and Mature Something............ 27

6. To Prepare is to Plan Over a Long Period 36

7. To Prepare is to Train for a Specific Task 40

8. To Prepare is to Lay a Foundation 44

9. To Prepare is to be Furnished with Scripture................. 54

10. To Prepare is to be Ready for War 58

11. To Prepare is to Put into a State of Readiness 66

12. To Prepare is to Set Your House in Order....................... 71

CHAPTER 1

The Art of Preparation

PREPARE THY WORK WITHOUT, and make it fit for thyself in the field; and afterwards build thine house.

Proverbs 24:27

Preparation is an art that can be learned. This book is intended to teach you about the skills, the discipline and the experiences you need in order to be prepared for your mission.

Jesus was the best example of someone who prepared for His mission. He prepared Himself for thirty years and ministered for only three years. Preparation is time consuming and that is why people try to avoid it. Quality preparation takes time!

All through the Bible, we are told to prepare for things and make ourselves ready. You even need to prepare to meet God. Therefore thus will I do unto thee, O Israel: and because I will do this unto thee, prepare to meet thy God, O Israel" (Amos 4:12). Let God impress upon your heart the need for you to make great preparations for your ministry.

You need to prepare for your preaching ministry.

You need to prepare for your apostolic ministry, where you will be planting and building churches.

You need to prepare for your prophetic ministry, where you will be speaking the Word of the Lord. Without studying history, you will not be a good prophet. Remember that that which has been is that which shall be!

You need to prepare for your pastoral ministry. There are many complex situations that will arise when you stay with one group of people for many years. There will be hurts and offences, there will be betrayals, there will be treachery, there will be disloyalty, there will be departures, there will be growth and there will be financial increase. There will be marriages, there will be broken relationships, there will be divorces, there will be deaths, there will be tragedies, there will be victories, there will be joy and there will be sorrow.

Every good leader and warrior needs to prepare for all these.

The art of preparation will make you thrive. It will make you confident in the face of every new challenge. Preparation will make you think about all the possibilities.

Preparation is all about getting yourself ready for what is to come. Preparation is getting yourself ready for your ministry unto the Lord. Indeed, those who prepare are easily distinguished from those who do not prepare. You must prepare for whatever work you do! Without preparation you will be slow and inefficient! Without preparation you will make mistakes! Without preparation you will lose favour!

With preparation, you will be smart and efficient! When you are well prepared, people will see you as an experienced and hardened warrior. Without adequate preparation you will always give off the impression that you are a "Johnny just come"!

Why Preparation?

1. **Preparation gives you an advantage over someone who has not prepared.** When you do not prepare, others will be chosen above you!

2. **The more you prepare, the more efficiently you can manage problems and overcome obstacles that will definitely arise.** Preparation makes you think ahead in order to have solutions for problems you have envisioned could arise. Without preparation you will spend your time reacting to problems rather than taking the initiative.

   Preparation helps you to deal with the challenges and problems that will arise. Everything that can go wrong will go wrong one day! Will you be ready to overcome the challenges that present themselves to you as you try to do the will of God? Jesus prepared for thirty years for His short ministry of three years. Jesus encountered many problems on earth. He overcame all of them because He was well prepared. All the fasting, all the prayer, all the waiting on God was part of His preparation.

3. **Preparation helps you to prevent anxiety and worry.** There is always stress when you are embarking on a new mission. The stress will be far less if you are prepared!

4. **Preparation prevents failure in any mission.** According to Benjamin Franklin, "By failing to prepare, you are preparing to fail!" There is nothing that cannot be achieved in God if you prepare for it adequately. Preparation allows you to relax, to flourish and to be confident in your mission.

Seven Things You Must Prepare For

1. **You must prepare for war. There will be wars! There will be battles! Prepare for them!**

   And next him was Jehozabad, AND WITH HIM AN HUNDRED AND FOURSCORE THOUSAND READY PREPARED FOR THE WAR. These waited on the king, beside those whom the king put in the fenced cities throughout all Judah.

   2 Chronicles 17:18-19

   The horse is prepared against the day of battle: but safety is of the Lord.

   Proverbs 21:31

2. **You must prepare for hard times.** There will be difficulties! There will be challenges! There will be pain! Prepare for these things! Hard times will surely come. Life is in seasons. You must be like the ant that prepares for hard times.

   The ants are a people not strong, YET THEY PREPARE THEIR MEAT IN THE SUMMER;

   Proverbs 30:25

3. **You must prepare to build the church. There will be projects!** There will be opportunities to build! There will be cities and nations that need church buildings! There will be countries that need to have churches! You must prepare to build the church! Make yourself ready! David prepared

4

abundantly to build the temple before he died. You must prepare to build the temple.

And David said, Solomon my son is young and tender, and the house that is to be builded for the Lord must be exceeding magnifical, of fame and of glory throughout all countries: I will therefore now make preparation for it. SO DAVID PREPARED ABUNDANTLY BEFORE HIS DEATH.

1 Chronicles 22:5

4. **You must prepare to seek God.** There will be opportunities to wait on God! There will be prayer meetings! There will be retreats! There will be church services! Make yourself ready to meet with the Lord!

And Jehoshaphat the king of Judah returned to his house in peace to Jerusalem. And Jehu the son of Hanani the seer went out to meet him, and said to king Jehoshaphat, Shouldest thou help the ungodly, and love them that hate the Lord? therefore is wrath upon thee from before the Lord. Nevertheless there are good things found in thee, in that thou hast taken away the groves out of the land, AND HAST PREPARED THINE HEART TO SEEK GOD.

2 Chronicles 19:1-3

It is a good thing to prepare your heart to seek the Lord. If you do not prepare your heart and your mind, you will not seek God. King Jehoshaphat prepared his heart to seek the Lord. You must prepare your heart to seek the Lord.

5. **You must prepare the way for the man of God.** There will be opportunities to be a John the Baptist who prepares the way of the Lord! Any ministry that has a preparation and advance team does better than those who just arrive on the scene. Jesus Christ had an "advance team" and his name was John the Baptist.

5

For this is he that was spoken of by the prophet Esaias, saying, The voice of one crying in the wilderness, PREPARE YE THE WAY OF THE LORD, MAKE HIS PATHS STRAIGHT.

Matthew 3:3

6. **You must prepare for the gospel.** You must prepare to preach the gospel of Jesus Christ. It takes years of preparation before you are ready to preach the gospel.

And your feet shod with the preparation of the gospel of peace;

Ephesians 6:15

7. **You must prepare to meet God.** There will be death! There will be funerals! There will be sorrow! There will be sudden and unexpected deaths! There will be slowly occurring deaths! Prepare for these things!

Therefore thus will I do unto thee, O Israel: and because I will do this unto thee, PREPARE TO MEET THY GOD, O ISRAEL.

Amos 4:12

CHAPTER 2

To Prepare is to Rehearse Ahead of Time

PREPARE THY WORK WITHOUT, and make it fit for thyself in the field; and afterwards build thine house.

Proverbs 24:27

A rehearsal is a practice session, which is usually private, in preparation for a public performance. God has many drill sessions of practice, waiting for you to go through. These drills or practice sessions, will prepare you for the big events that are in your future.

Rehearsals are always an important form of preparation. Rehearsals can be boring! Without rehearsals you will not do well at the big event. There are many things that cannot be prepared for unless we prepare for them by having a rehearsal. You simply have to go through something a few times in order to make yourself ready for the big event. You cannot sing a song well without rehearsing it over and over. You cannot be a great singer without many rehearsals. You need to have had private bad experiences on the stage in order to overcome them in the future. You can always tell an experienced singer from an inexperienced one. Experienced singers rarely get into trouble on stage because they have already had many private rehearsals.

Rehearsals will privately prepare you for the big event. Do not be discouraged when bad things happen during your rehearsal. Thank God it is just a rehearsal! There are great days and great events ahead!

1. To prepare is to rehearse your fighting skills.

There are many battles lined up for you in the ministry. Get ready to become a fighter! Get ready to win! Get ready to overcome! The Lord is going to reward you for the things you overcame. David had private rehearsals ahead of time.

To prepare is to rehearse ahead of time. David rehearsed by fighting with a lion. David rehearsed by fighting with a bear. Finally the great day came and he was fighting with Goliath. His fight with Goliath earned him the great reputation that he carried throughout his ministry. A reputation is sometimes earned in a day. One great event can earn you a lifetime reputation!

God is going to prepare you for the biggest battles that lie ahead by giving you some smaller ones to fight today. You will experience a fight with a bear and a lion. By defeating them, you would have had a good rehearsal for the fight with a monster.

Do not be discouraged about the many battles you are experiencing. They are all to prepare you for the big one ahead. I have seen many things in the ministry; many battles, many sorrows and many tears. Each of those fights was earning me some readiness and giving me some skills for future battles.

AND DAVID SAID TO SAUL, LET NO MAN'S HEART FAIL BECAUSE OF HIM; THY SERVANT WILL GO AND FIGHT WITH THIS PHILISTINE. And Saul said to David, Thou art not able to go against this Philistine to fight with him: for thou art but a youth, and he a man of war from his youth. And David said unto Saul, THY SERVANT KEPT HIS FATHER'S SHEEP, AND THERE CAME A LION, AND A BEAR, AND TOOK A LAMB OUT OF THE FLOCK: AND I WENT OUT AFTER HIM, AND SMOTE HIM, AND DELIVERED IT OUT OF HIS MOUTH: and when he arose against me, I caught him by his beard, and smote him, and slew him. Thy servant slew both the lion and the bear: and this uncircumcised Philistine shall be as one of them, seeing he hath defied the armies of the living God. David said moreover, The Lord that delivered me out of the paw of the lion, and out of the paw of the bear, he will deliver me out of the hand of this Philistine. And Saul said unto David, Go, and the Lord be with thee.

1 Samuel 17:32-37

2.   To prepare is to rehearse your shepherding skills.

Wheresoever I have walked with all Israel, spake I a word to any of the judges of Israel, whom I commanded to feed my people, saying, Why have ye not built me an house of cedars? Now therefore thus shalt thou say unto my servant David, Thus saith the Lord of hosts, I TOOK THEE FROM THE SHEEPCOTE, EVEN

FROM FOLLOWING THE SHEEP, THAT THOU SHOULDEST BE RULER OVER MY PEOPLE ISRAEL: And I have been with thee whithersoever thou hast walked, and have cut off all thine enemies from before thee, and have made thee a name like the name of the great men that are in the earth.

1 Chronicles 17:6-8

King David rehearsed how to look after people by looking after sheep. David's private experiences with sheep were his preparation for looking after God's people. Looking after people is an art. Being a shepherd involves a lot of skill. It is easy to tell the difference between a young shepherd and an old shepherd. Young shepherds are moved very quickly and easily by people's problems. Older shepherds are not quickly impressed or deceived by people. There are sheep that I have wept over and poured out my bowels and entrails for, only to find out that they were deceiving me. As I became an older shepherd, I was not so easily deceived by deceivers.

There are funerals I have attended where I cried and was so moved by the event, only to discover a few years later that there was actually nothing to cry about. Younger shepherds are more easily deceived. God allows you to go through different experiences as a rehearsal for things to come. You must not shy away from looking after the smallest, youngest, most insignificant person. Each person you care for is a rehearsal for the day you become the shepherd of the president of your country.

3. **To prepare is to rehearse your preaching skills.**

Then he called his twelve disciples together, and gave them power and authority over all devils, and to cure diseases. And he sent them to preach the kingdom of God, and to heal the sick. And he said unto them, Take nothing for your journey, neither staves, nor scrip, neither bread, neither money; neither have two coats apiece. And whatsoever house ye enter into,

there abide, and thence depart. And whosoever will not receive you, when ye go out of that city, shake off the very dust from your feet for a testimony against them. And they departed, and went through the towns, preaching the gospel, and healing every where.

Luke 9:1-6

But ye shall receive power, after that the Holy Ghost is come upon you: and ye shall be witnesses unto me both in Jerusalem, and in all Judaea, and in Samaria, and unto the uttermost part of the earth.

Acts 1:8

The missions that Jesus sent His disciples on were actually private practice sessions. The disciples rehearsed their preaching ministry when they were sent out by the Lord. Later on, these same disciples were sent out into the world to preach the gospel. Jesus had afforded them the opportunity to rehearse their preaching. Preaching is an art! You will need private drills to perfect your skills!   God is going to give you larger and larger platforms from which to minister the word of God. Every small church and small group I have ever ministered to, has been a preparation for a larger one.

You will rehearse how to start a message and you will rehearse how to stop preaching. You will rehearse how to preach for a long time and also how to preach for a short time. You will rehearse how to preach to those who "know it all" and you will also rehearse how to preach to innocent hungry souls. You will learn how to preach with an interpreter and you will learn how to preach without an interpreter.

You will learn how to preach to people who have no expression on their faces whatsoever, and you will learn how to preach to those who shout "Amen" and "Yes, Lord". You will learn how to preach in the dry season and this will be a rehearsal for preaching in the rain.

Preaching needs rehearsals and God is going to give you as many rehearsals as you need. Never say "No" to the opportunity to preach. To prepare is to rehearse ahead of time!

One day I found myself in a stadium with a hundred thousand people. It was time to preach the word of God and pray for the sick. I had been rehearsing this very thing with much smaller groups. All I had to do was to do what I had been doing in the smaller groups. Preaching to a hundred people became preaching to a hundred thousand people! Do not forget to take every opportunity to minister the word of God.

4. To prepare is to rehearse your healing ministry.

Then he called his twelve disciples together, and gave them power and authority over all devils, and to cure diseases. And he sent them to preach the kingdom of God, and to heal the sick.

Luke 9:1-2

Jesus allowed His disciples to rehearse their healing ministries. That is why He sent them out to cure diseases and to cast out devils. It is important to rehearse your healing ministry. I have prayed for the sick in many different circumstances. Looking back, I realise that each opportunity I had to pray for the sick was a rehearsal for greater days ahead. One day I was preaching to a group of about twenty people and I felt the Lord telling me that I really needed to pray for the sick.

I really did not want to pray for the sick because there were so few people present. As I preached, I could not get away from the conviction to pray for people. Indeed, I felt I would be in danger if I did not obey God.

Finally, I prayed for the sick and a man who had been blind in one eye came forward to testify that he had been blind for many years in one eye but was totally healed. I could not believe my eyes as this man testified. I realised that God had given me a great rehearsal for other days where I would see many other blind people healed.

Do not run away from the opportunity to pray for the sick. Every testimony of headaches being healed is a rehearsal for hearing bigger testimonies one day. You will learn how to pray for the sick in the dry season and you will learn to pray for the sick in the rainy season.

One day, I was having a crusade and it began to rain. I thought that no one would be healed because it was raining; but I still felt the need to pray for the sick. After praying for the sick there were many testimonies. Then I realised that God was a God of the rainy season as well as a God of the dry season.

Some years later, I was on a much larger crusade platform and it began to rain. I knew immediately that I would still pray for the sick and there would be miracles because I had had one rehearsal in the rain. My rehearsal paid off and many people were healed.

Do not shy away from the many rehearsals that God is giving you for your ministry. God is going to use you mightily but you need many rehearsals.

One day, I was about to preach when the president of the country walked in. He sat behind me throughout my preaching and watched me pray for the sick.

Throughout that evening, I simply did what I was used to doing in many other rehearsals. God had prepared me for the day when the president of a country would be sitting behind me with all his ministers and security men. Do not shy away from the many rehearsals of your healing ministry!

5. To prepare is to rehearse living by faith.

And he said unto them, Take nothing for your journey, neither staves, nor scrip, neither bread, neither money; neither have two coats apiece. And whatsoever house

ye enter into, there abide, and thence depart. And whosoever will not receive you, when ye go out of that city, shake off the very dust from your feet for a testimony against them.

Luke 9:3-5

And he said unto them, When I sent you without purse, and scrip, and shoes, lacked ye any thing? And they said, Nothing.

Luke 22:35

Jesus allowed His disciples to rehearse what it meant to have faith in God for provision. You will need to rehearse living by faith. Jesus taught His disciples to go out and trust God for finances. Jesus sent them without purse and without money. When the disciples came back, He asked them, "Did you lack anything?" Jesus had just given them a great lesson in surviving by faith. You may be in Bible school. God will give you a lesson on faith and on how to overcome financial problems.

Finances will always be a challenge for the ministry. Never think that churches anywhere have all the money that they need. Many churches are actually in debt, scrounging for scraps from day to day. We will always have to trust God to provide our needs.

When you are young in ministry, God gives you a chance to rehearse a life of trusting Him. To live off a salary takes a lot of faith! To live without a salary involves a high level of faith! To prosper without earning a regular salary also involves a lot of faith. All these levels of ministry involve rehearsals. Learn to trust God and He will take care of all your needs!

6. To prepare is to rehearse living amongst wolves.

Go your ways: behold, I send you forth as lambs among wolves.

Luke 10:3

Jesus is sending us out as sheep amongst wolves. There will always be wolves amongst us who want to devour us. There will always be girls who want to sleep with you. There will always be boys who want to sleep with you. Every experience you have with the opposite sex is a rehearsal for wilder experiences that God is training you for.

If you have defeated one wolf before, you may be more confident when you see another. Your rehearsal with the earlier wolf will actually teach you how to recognise wolves and how to fight them. There is a proverb that says that "A dishonourable man can only deceive an innocent girl once."

Throughout your ministry you will encounter liars and thieves. You will also encounter Judases, Joabs and Absaloms. It is important that you learn to fight them and overcome them.

Satan does not have many new tricks. He keeps on repeating the old ones. If you do not learn enough about satan's old tricks, he will lazily repeat the same things that destroyed others who came just before you.

You will not be destroyed when God gives you rehearsals to prepare you!

Every lecherous man and every lustful woman you have ever encountered will be a rehearsal for future interactions with wolves. Receive the power to overcome wolves because you are being sent forth as lambs in the midst of wolves.

7. To prepare is to rehearse surviving rejection and overcoming failure.

But into whatsoever city ye enter, and they receive you not, go your ways out into the streets of the same, and say, Even the very dust of your city, which cleaveth on us, we do wipe off against you: notwithstanding be ye sure of this, that the kingdom of God is come nigh unto you.

Luke 10:10-11

You will also be given the opportunity to rehearse rejection and failure. Jesus sent His disciples to places where they would not be received. Not everyone will receive you and not everyone will accept you. There are some missions that will not be successful. Jesus knew that not every mission would work. That is why He taught them how to shake the dust off their feet.

Do not be discouraged with failure. Some of the failures are rehearsals to keep you strengthened for other greater failures that are coming down the road. Many people will reject you before you are accepted. In many instances, a person is not accepted until he is first rejected.

You must encounter ridicule, criticism, accusation and rejection as part of your calling. God knew that people would reject Jesus Christ but He sent Jesus into the world. Just as Jesus was sent into the world to be rejected, you are being sent into the world to be rejected. Every rejection and every failure is a rehearsal to strengthen you so that you do not fail in the next big test.

CHAPTER 3

To Prepare is to
Foresee Problems

A prudent man foreseeth the evil, and hideth himself:
but the simple pass on, and are punished.

Proverbs 22:3

Foreseeing problems is an important part of preparation. As a minister of God, it is important to foresee the problems that you will encounter. How can you foresee the problems you will encounter? All you have to do is to read and study and you will discover the problems you will encounter.

1. **You can foresee the problems of those who are sent by analysing the problems of someone who was sent before you.**

    Then said Jesus to them again, Peace be unto you: as my Father hath sent me, even so send I you.

    John 20:21

    Jesus was sent into the world to preach the gospel and to do the will of God. Just as Jesus was sent into this wicked world, we have been sent into the same world. We have been sent to walk in His footsteps and to do greater works. What did Jesus experience? How was His love repaid? Was He appreciated? Was He encouraged? Was He deserted? Was He abandoned by those He loved? Was He betrayed by the closest of all? Indeed, you are not greater than your master. If Jesus experienced all these things, you will surely experience the same. The closer you get to Jesus, the more your experiences will mimic His.

2. **You can foresee problems of ministry by analysing the problems that Apostle Paul had.** The problems of Apostle Paul give you a picture of the kind of problems you should expect as an apostle. Has God called you to be a great apostle? I foresee afflictions, necessities, distresses, stripes, imprisonments, labours, tumults, watchings and fastings. Looking at the life of Apostle Paul will help you to foresee the problems ahead.

    Giving no offence in any thing, that the ministry be not blamed: But in all things approving ourselves as the ministers of God, in much patience, in afflictions, in necessities, in distresses, In stripes, in imprisonments, in tumults, in labours, in watchings, in fastings; By pureness, by knowledge, by longsuffering, by kindness, by the Holy Ghost, by love unfeigned, By the word

of truth, by the power of God, by the armour of righteousness on the right hand and on the left, By honour and dishonour, by evil report and good report: as deceivers, and yet true; As unknown, and yet well known; as dying, and, behold, we live; as chastened, and not killed; As sorrowful, yet alway rejoicing; as poor, yet making many rich; as having nothing, and yet possessing all things.

2 Corinthians 6:3-10

3. **You can foresee the problems of an apostle by analysing the problems that apostles have had.** What are the problems that Jesus' disciples had? They had problems of being made spectacles to the world and to men. The disciples of Jesus were ridiculed and considered as fools for Christ's sake. Expect to be despised and rejected. Are you going into real ministry? Or are you going into a fake ministry? You must expect hunger, thirst, nakedness and no certain dwelling place. Do not be concerned if you are made into the offscouring of this world.

For I think that God hath set forth us the apostles last, as it were appointed to death: for we are made a spectacle unto the world, and to angels, and to men. We are fools for Christ's sake, but ye are wise in Christ; we are weak, but ye are strong; ye are honourable, but we are despised.
Even unto this present hour we both hunger, and thirst, and are naked, and are buffeted, and have no certain dwellingplace; And labour, working with our own hands: being reviled, we bless; being persecuted, we suffer it: Being defamed, we intreat: we are made as the filth of the world, and are the offscouring of all things unto this day. I write not these things to shame you, but as my beloved sons I warn you. For though ye have ten thousand instructors in Christ, yet have ye not many fathers: for in Christ Jesus I have begotten you through the gospel.

1 Corinthians 4:9-15

4. You can foresee problems by studying history.

The thing that hath been, it is that which shall be; and that which is done is that which shall be done: and there is no new thing under the sun.

Ecclesiastes 1:9

What has happened before, is what will happen again! The problems that your predecessors saw are the problems that you will also see. The difficulties that your predecessors experienced are the difficulties you will experience. There is simply nothing new under the sun.

The study of biographies is the study of history. The study of the life of Moses reveals many intriguing details. Studying books like *"God's Generals"*[1] will reveal to you the kind of problems a general is going to have.

5. To foresee problems is to expect surprises.

Kerioth is taken, and the strong holds are surprised, and the mighty men's hearts in Moab at that day shall be as the heart of a woman in her pangs. And Moab shall be destroyed from being a people, because he hath magnified himself against the Lord.

Jeremiah 48:41-42

There will be surprises! One of the attacks of the enemy is to surprise you. Without the element of surprise, many attacks of the enemy will not work.

There are many things you must do in order to overcome surprises. Pilots of aeroplanes and captains of ships are always on the lookout for surprises. There will be surprises! There will be things you do not expect! God will be with you, but you must expect surprises!

---

[1] *Liardon, Roberts. God's Generals: Why They Succeeded and Why They Failed (Vol 1), Whitaker House, 1996*

CHAPTER 4

To Prepare is to Educate Yourself with Special Knowledge

Study to shew thyself approved unto God, a workman that needeth not to be ashamed, rightly dividing the word of truth.

2 Timothy 2:15

1. **Prepare for the gospel by educating yourself with special knowledge about the ministry.**

    Paul, an apostle of Jesus Christ by the commandment of God our Saviour, and Lord Jesus Christ, which is our hope; Unto Timothy, my own son in the faith: Grace, mercy, and peace, from God our Father and Jesus Christ our Lord. As I besought thee to abide still at Ephesus, when I went into Macedonia, that thou mightest charge some that they teach no other doctrine, Neither give heed to fables and endless genealogies, which minister questions, rather than godly edifying which is in faith: so do.

    1 Timothy 1:1-4

    You must study books about the ministry! You cannot just read newspapers if you want to be a minister.

    Apostle Paul taught many things about the ministry. This was necessary because not everybody was qualified to hear what he had to say about ministry. There are things that Apostle Paul wrote specifically to a minister of the gospel. He wrote letters that we call First Timothy, Second Timothy and Titus. Those books contain the special knowledge that is needed for ministry. Educating yourself with these books is key to preparing for the gospel of Jesus Christ. Every man of God must study books in the Bible that are specially related to ministers.

2. **Prepare for the gospel by educating yourself with special knowledge from books and parchments.**

    The cloke that I left at Troas with Carpus, when thou comest, bring with thee, and the books, but especially the parchments.

    2 Timothy 4:13

    Every minister must have special books that he uses to educate himself with special knowledge. This special knowledge is needed for ministry. Apostle Paul was very concerned about getting his books and parchments. These books and parchments were critical to his ministry. They contained special knowledge about the ministry. Of all the things that he had left behind, he was concerned about getting his books and parchments. The books and parchments of a man of God are his most treasured possession. Through books and parchments, you receive special information that will guide you.

One day, I was waiting on the Lord in another country. I sought the Lord to heal me of my troubles that I had encountered by virtue of the fact that I was in the ministry. I was experiencing the "fires" of affliction and troubles that would not go away.

The house in which I was staying had a beautiful open balcony from where I could see all that was happening downstairs. A bookshelf that was downstairs caught my eye. The house was quiet because there was nobody at home. I decided to walk down to the bookshelf to see the books that were on the shelf. At the time, I was despondent and discouraged about everything in the ministry. The book that I opened had special knowledge about the ministry. I received a lot of comfort and direction by reading that strange book from the shelf. Those are the kinds of books you need if you want to educate yourself with special knowledge. You need special books to educate you!

3. Prepare yourself for the gospel by educating yourself with special knowledge on the anointing.

The Spirit of the Lord is upon me, because he hath anointed me to preach the gospel to the poor; he hath sent me to heal the brokenhearted, to preach deliverance to the captives, and recovering of sight to the blind, to set at liberty them that are bruised,

Luke 4:18

The first time Jesus ever preached, He spoke about the anointing. Jesus Christ was very deep into the subject of the anointing. The anointing is the power with which you do ministry. Without the anointing, you cannot do very much!

Without the anointing you cannot even be a minister. Jesus' first topic when He began the ministry was to speak about the anointing and what it meant to Him. The anointing does not mean much for those who are not ministering the gospel.

The Holy Spirit is a boring subject for those who are not in the ministry. But for those of us who are in the ministry, the Holy Spirit by Himself, is an education in special knowledge.

4. Prepare yourself for the gospel by educating yourself with special knowledge on the art of leadership.

Every minister is a leader of some sort. Many people are poor leaders. A leader is a captain of a ship. There is a special grace and anointing for leadership. Saul, an errand boy for his father, was anointed to be a captain over God's people.

Samuel took a small jar of olive oil and poured it on Saul's head. Then he kissed Saul and told him: The Lord has chosen you to be the leader and ruler of his people.

1 Samuel 10:1 (CEV)

There is also special wisdom that is needed to be a leader. You need to seek that wisdom and learn all that there is to learn about leadership. Kings and princes rule through that special wisdom for leadership. Incompetent kings are a danger to the people they lead as well as a danger to themselves. It is so sad to see nations with incompetent leaders at the helm of affairs. These leaders are a danger to themselves and a danger to the people they lead.

Counsel is mine, and sound wisdom: I am understanding; I have strength. BY ME KINGS REIGN, and princes decree justice.

Proverbs 8:14-15

It is so sad to see ships that have incompetent captains. Incompetent leaders are a danger to the people they lead as well as a danger to themselves. It is so sad to see churches with

24

incompetent leaders at the helm of affairs. These leaders are a danger to themselves and a danger to the people they lead.

5. **Prepare yourself for the gospel by educating yourself with special knowledge about warfare.**

   Fight the good fight of faith, lay hold on eternal life, whereunto thou art also called, and hast professed a good profession before many witnesses.

   1 Timothy 6:12

Apostle Paul said to Timothy, "You need to fight a good fight." He did not say that to ordinary Christians. He said that to Timothy the pastor.

Being a Christian is war! But being a minister of the gospel is a series of ultimate wars, firestorms, noisy battles, agonizing screams and losses mixed with victories.

It is important to understand how to fight the enemy. It is important to understand where the enemy is! It is important to understand who the enemy is! Fighting a war is no mean undertaking. You certainly need to be educated with special knowledge about warfare.

There are even special prophecies for ministers.

   This charge I commit unto thee, son Timothy, according to the prophecies which went before on thee, that thou by them mightest war a good warfare;

   1 Timothy 1:18

To prepare for the gospel, you need to be educated with special knowledge about war in the heavenlies and about fighting dragons. You need to know more about the spirit world and how to fight the beings that exist just beyond human vision. A minister of the gospel is stuck in a battle that is going on in the heavenlies for the souls of men. Every time you are insulted, ridiculed, intimidated and mocked, it is because there are spirits of blasphemy operating against you in the heavenlies. You need special knowledge about spiritual serpents, spiritual dragons, spiritual flies and spiritual horses that operate in the heavenlies. You need to be educated with special knowledge about angels who help you in your battle.

> And there was war in heaven: Michael and his angels fought against the dragon; and the dragon fought and his angels, and prevailed not; neither was their place found any more in heaven. And the great dragon was cast out, that old serpent, called the Devil, and Satan, which deceiveth the whole world: he was cast out into the earth, and his angels were cast out with him.
>
> Revelation 12:7-9

CHAPTER 5

To Prepare is to Mellow and Mature Something

Ephraim, he hath mixed himself among the people;
EPHRAIM IS A CAKE NOT TURNED.

Hosea 7:8

66 **A** cake not turned" is a cake that is not ready to be eaten. It needs to mature! It needs to mellow! It needs to ripen! An important aspect of preparation is when you are made to mature and to become mellow. Maturity is the ripened stage of ministry. Maturity is the end-stage of a normal developmental process.

When you are mature, you have come to your stage of full development.

To mellow something is to make it soft, sweet and fully flavoured. God wants to make you fully flavoured for the ministry!

When you are mellowed, you have been made gentle and compassionate by age and experience.

A minister of the gospel must become gentle and compassionate through experience. The immature disciples of Christ were ready to kill everyone who did not comply with their teachings. Jesus was preparing the disciples by mellowing them and maturing them for real life and ministry.

And sent messengers before his face: and they went, and entered into a village of the Samaritans, to make ready for him. And they did not receive him, because his face was as though he would go to Jerusalem. AND WHEN HIS DISCIPLES JAMES AND JOHN SAW THIS, THEY SAID, LORD, WILT THOU THAT WE COMMAND FIRE TO COME DOWN FROM HEAVEN, AND CONSUME THEM, EVEN AS ELIAS DID? But he turned, and rebuked them, and said, ye know not what manner of spirit ye are of. For the Son of man is not come to destroy men's lives, but to save them. And they went to another village.

Luke 9:52-56

Idealistic people are quick to condemn others. Inexperienced people are very strict and unforgiving with human weakness.

Mature and mellow ministers are very different. Notice Jesus' response towards the woman caught in adultery. Notice that Jesus did not condemn this adulterous lady, although the Pharisees did (John 8: 3-11). Notice Jesus' response to the woman of Samaria. He turned her into an evangelist even though she had had five husbands (John 4:5-29).

Perhaps you are not able to turn people into evangelists because you are not mature and mellow in ministry. A mellow and mature minister will know that it is very easy for a woman to have more than five men in her life. Jesus turned this woman of Samaria into the first evangelist of the church. An evangelist is someone who proclaims the news about Jesus Christ. This woman became the first person to proclaim the news about Jesus Christ.

Many servants of God are yet to become gentle, fully developed and ripened for ministry. It is time to complete your development and preparation for ministry.

When a person is mature, he is experienced in such a way that completes his development. Apostle Paul said he was striving to know God and to know the fellowship of His suffering. Why would this great apostle who wrote half of the New Testament still be striving to know God and the fellowship of His sufferings? Indeed, it takes time to even know and understand the God we are serving and following.

That I may know him, and the power of his resurrection, and the fellowship of his sufferings, being made conformable unto his death; If by any means I might attain unto the resurrection of the dead.

Philippians 3:10-11

How to Become Mature and Mellow

Cursed be he that doeth the work of the Lord deceitfully, and cursed be he that keepeth back his

29

sword from blood. MOAB HATH BEEN AT EASE FROM HIS YOUTH, AND HE HATH SETTLED ON HIS LEES, and hath not been emptied from vessel to vessel, neither hath he gone into captivity: therefore his taste remained in him, and his scent is not changed.

Jeremiah 48:10-11

Many ministers are not complete in their development as men of God. It takes many years to mature and to mellow into what God wants you to be.

The scripture describes very well the immature nature of Moab. Moab was at ease and relaxed in his condition. Moab was compared to wine that was not mature. Wine is supposed to taste nicer when it is mature and mellow. The older the wine and the more mature the wine, the more expensive it is.

In this scripture, the Lord gives the master keys to maturing and mellowing Moab. Moab had become prematurely settled and relaxed, failing to become what God wanted him to become. In this amazing scripture (Jeremiah 48:10-11), there are many characteristics that we see of an immature person who has not become what God wants him to be.

1. **To mellow and mature, you must not be at allowed to be at ease.**

   It is good for a man that he bear the yoke in his youth.
   Lamentations 3:27

To be at ease is to be at rest! Resting, sleeping and taking it easy are not the ways to mature in life and ministry. A girl who rests, sleeps and takes it easy in her youth, will not learn how to cook. She will have no domestic skills and will enter marriage as an unskilled person.

It is important to rise up and bear the yoke of ministry, doing the hard things that are necessary to develop your skills. Be an usher, be a security man, run around, go out witnessing and serve the Lord in every possible way. By working hard you mature very quickly into ministry.

30

2. To mellow and mature, you must not be settled in any place.

And it shall come to pass at that time, THAT I WILL SEARCH JERUSALEM WITH CANDLES, AND PUNISH THE MEN THAT ARE SETTLED ON THEIR LEES: that say in their heart, The Lord will not do good, neither will he do evil.

Zephaniah 1:12

To become settled in anything is to end the process of maturity. Many of us want to be settled, established and even exalted. But there is a certain tension that is necessary if you are to mature in ministry. Living in a big house, driving a big car and flying around in business and first class are not the ways to maturity.

3. To mellow and mature, you must be emptied from vessel to vessel.

Moab hath been at ease from his youth, and he hath settled on his lees, and HATH NOT BEEN EMPTIED FROM VESSEL TO VESSEL, neither hath he gone into captivity: therefore his taste remained in him, and his scent is not changed.

Jeremiah 48:11

You must go from place to place. You must move from experience to experience. In order to mature the wine, it is poured from vessel to vessel. You must be sent from place to place. You must move from country to country. You must move from church to church, becoming active in every new opportunity you are given.

Come now therefore, and I will send thee unto Pharaoh, that thou mayest bring forth my people the children of Israel out of Egypt. And Moses said unto God, Who am I, that I should go unto Pharaoh, and that I should bring forth the children of Israel out of Egypt?

Exodus 3:10-11

31

Moses was matured and mellowed through the experience he had had in the wilderness. By the time he had been emptied from the wilderness back to Egypt, he was a completely different person. When God called him, he declined the call. He said he was not worthy. In his immature state earlier, he had been ready to kill a man to accomplish the purposes of God (Exodus 2:11-12).

Joseph was equally immature when God first approached him. He told everyone that he was going to become a star, someone that everyone would bow down to. He provoked his brothers with his calling and set off a chain reaction that led him to captivity. By the time he came out of captivity, Joseph was far more mature.

Whilst Joseph was in prison, he asked another prisoner to remember him. Someone who is asking to be remembered or promoted is not yet ready to be used by God. It took another two years before Joseph was released from prison.

In all, Joseph spent one year in Potiphar's house and twelve years in prison. When he had gone through the experience of being completely forgotten by man, he was ready to be set free. Joseph was emptied from vessel to vessel several times. He was emptied from the land of Canaan to the Midianites, and from the Midianites to the Ishmaelites and from the Ishmaelites to Potiphar's house and from Potiphar's house to the prison! By the time he came out of the prison he was completely mellowed and matured. He was not the kind of person who would exact revenge on his brothers. This is all that God was trying to accomplish in the heart of Joseph. Remember that God is trying to mellow and mature you.

4. To mellow and mature, you must experience captivity, bondage and restrictions.

Moab hath been at ease from his youth, and he hath settled on his lees, and hath not been emptied from

vessel to vessel, NEITHER HATH HE GONE INTO CAPTIVITY: THEREFORE HIS TASTE REMAINED IN HIM, AND HIS SCENT IS NOT CHANGED.

Jeremiah 48:11

Maturity also comes when you enter into captivity. There are many restrictions that you will experience on your way to maturity. Being stuck under an oppressive leader is a common type of captivity. Being in a relationship with a father may be difficult and challenging and is yet another type of captivity. Marriage is one of the restrictions and forms of captivity that a minister can experience.

When you have been in captivity, you become a mature minister of the gospel. The scripture just before shows us that captivity is one of the ways to becoming mellow and mature. Do not run away from the captivity that God gives to you. There are things that you will not like but you will be forced to do. Apostle Peter was told by Jesus, "One day someone will carry you where you do not want to go". Peter was not happy to hear this and began to ask questions about John (John 21:19-22).

Verily, verily, I say unto thee, When thou wast young, thou girdedst thyself, and walkedst whither thou wouldest: but when thou shalt be old, thou shalt stretch forth thy hands, and another shall gird thee, and carry thee whither thou wouldest not.

John 21:18

There is nothing like maturity without captivity. Captivity is a necessary stage to your full maturity and development. It is important to accept captivity and restrictions. There are many restrictions for a minister. You cannot just live anyhow. You cannot just do what you like and what you want. You must do what God wants. You cannot just have the friends you want to have or any relationship you want to have. You cannot have the things you want to have. You must have the things that God wants and the people that God wants in your life. Is it not surprising that it is a mature person who quietly allows himself to be carried along?

5. To mellow and mature, your taste must change.

And the cares of this world, and the deceitfulness of riches, and the lusts of other things entering in, choke the word, and it becometh unfruitful.

Mark 4:19

Many ministers have desires and tastes for other things. These desires and tastes destroy them along the line. Part of your preparation for the ministry is to wipe out your desires for other things.

You must wipe out your desires for the things that you do not need. There are things that must not be part of your life and ministry. This is why the Lord said that the taste of Moab had not changed. His taste remained in him (Jeremiah 48:11). God wants you to develop a taste for good, heavenly and spiritual things.

Your tastes speak of the things you like. Your desires and your longings must shift. When you are younger, you have the desire for certain cars, houses and even countries. As you mature and mellow, these tastes will change.

Many people have trouble in their ministry because at the time they were getting married, they had a taste for troublesome women. Their tastes were centred around the colour of the skin, whether the girl was golden brown or ebony black. Some people just wanted a fair-coloured person. Some people wanted someone with smooth skin. Some people were looking for a face without pimples. Such tastes will change as you mature and mellow. A mature person will not be very concerned about such things. A mature and mellow person will look for peace, compliance and humility in a woman. What is the use of ebony black, golden brown and coffee-coloured women if they are not humble and flowing? How will it help us? Why should you enter a river and complain afterwards that it is too deep or too cold?

6. To mellow and mature, your scent must change.

For we are unto God a sweet savour of Christ, in them that are saved, and in them that perish: To the one we are the savour of death unto death; and to the other the savour of life unto life. And who is sufficient for these things?

2 Corinthians 2:15-16

In ministry, your scent must change! Every minister gives off a certain scent. Paul calls it the "savour" of ministry. Every minister gives off a certain feeling, sensation and scent! There are some people who give off the scent of the country they are from. Some people give off the scent of the tribe they come from. Once you are in their presence you become aware of these things without knowing why. Paul called it the "savour" of the gospel.

What kind of scent do you have? What kind of feelings do you exude? When people are around you, what do they feel? Do they feel the love of God? Do they feel spirituality? Do they feel the anointing?

I know some people who exude an air of intelligence. Some people give you a feeling that you are with a professor. Some people give you a feeling that you are with a philosopher. Yet others give you the feeling of being with a spiritual person whose head is in the clouds and who is thinking about spiritual things.

There are some men of God who give you a feeling of prideful intelligence and there are others who give you a feeling of humility. There are also others who exude a confidence that is pride in its most basic form.

CHAPTER 6

To Prepare is to Plan Over a Long Period

Forasmuch as ye know that ye were not redeemed with corruptible things, as silver and gold, from your vain conversation received by tradition from your fathers; But with the precious blood of Christ, as of a lamb without blemish and without spot: WHO VERILY WAS FOREORDAINED BEFORE THE FOUNDATION OF THE WORLD, but was manifest in these last times for you, Who by him do believe in God, that raised him up from the dead, and gave him glory; that your faith and hope might be in God.

1 Peter 1:18-21

G od has a plan that He will implement and no matter how long it takes, His plan is going to come to pass.

God planned this gospel a long time ago before the foundation of the world. You must also plan over a long period to do the will of God. Many people take emotional decisions about serving God. They may be in a church service and become emotionally charged up. After a while, these emotions die down and they feel that they made a mistake in saying, "Yes" to the call of God.

The preparation of the gospel involves planning over a long period. It does not involve having a short emotional hype that fizzles out after three weeks. It is time to plan over a long period that you will serve God. It is time to plan over a long period to be a missionary. How do you plan over a long period?

1. **Plan over a long period by believing in your childhood dreams and visions.** Your childhood callings are part of the long-term planning that God is preparing you with.

    Before I formed thee in the belly I knew thee; and before thou camest forth out of the womb I sanctified thee, and I ordained thee a prophet unto the nations. Then said I, Ah, Lord God! behold, I cannot speak: for I am a child. But the Lord said unto me, Say not, I am a child: for thou shalt go to all that I shall send thee, and whatsoever I command thee thou shalt speak. Be not afraid of their faces: for I am with thee to deliver thee, saith the Lord.

    Jeremiah 1:5-8

2. **Plan over a long period by having well thought through plans for ministry.**

    Forasmuch then as Christ hath suffered for us in the flesh, arm yourselves likewise with the same mind: for he that hath suffered in the flesh hath ceased from sin;
    1 Peter 4:1

Preparing for the ministry involves arming yourself with the right mind. When you have thought through your sacrifice, you are more able to go through the pain and disadvantage that will come to you because of it.

You can prepare for your ministry by thinking carefully about all that God has called you to do. You must also think about what the ministry is going to mean for your family. People do not think though their plans. That is why they become bitter in the middle of the road. You must analyse the call of God and what sacrifices you are going to be called upon to make for God.

What is ministry going to mean for your children? What is it going to mean for your future? What is it going to mean for you financially? What other options do you have? Will you be better off working somewhere else? Some people are actually better off in the ministry but do not think through the realities. Many people would be better off living on the mission field than in their home country. They just assume that living in America must be better than living anywhere else. It is time to arm yourself by having the right mind.

3. **Plan over a long period by setting your heart on the visions of God.**

   And the man said unto me, SON OF MAN, BEHOLD WITH THINE EYES, AND HEAR WITH THINE EARS, AND SET THINE HEART UPON ALL THAT I SHALL SHEW THEE; for to the intent that I might shew them unto thee art thou brought hither: declare all that thou seest to the house of Israel.

   Ezekiel 40:4

When God reveals something to you, set your heart on it. Open your eyes and open your ears to the word of God. As God speaks to you, set your heart on it. As you set your heart on it, it will surely come to pass. It is only when your heart is fixed on the purpose of God that you will fulfil the will of God.

4. Plan over a long period of time by expecting a long wait.

And the Lord answered me, and said, Write the vision, and make it plain upon tables, that he may run that readeth it. For the vision is yet for an appointed time, but at the end it shall speak, and not lie: THOUGH IT TARRY, WAIT FOR IT; BECAUSE IT WILL SURELY COME, IT WILL NOT TARRY.

Habakkuk 2:2-3

You must understand that the purposes of God are something that you have to wait for. Do not despair when the visions of God seem to be delaying. They will surely come to pass. To prepare for the gospel is to plan over a long period of time. To plan ahead is to be ready to wait for as long as it takes.

CHAPTER 7

To Prepare is to Train for a Specific Task

And Jesus went about all the cities and villages, teaching in their synagogues, and preaching the gospel of the kingdom, and healing every sickness and every disease among the people.

Matthew 9:35

T he preparation of the gospel means that you are going to be trained for a specific task.

Those who work for God are trained for specific tasks. You are not being trained to become a bank manager. You are being trained for a specific task, the task of preaching and teaching the word of God. You are being trained on what to preach, where to preach and how to preach!

1. **You are being trained in the art of preaching and teaching. Jesus Christ was a preacher like no other.**

    Then came the officers to the chief priests and Pharisees; and they said unto them, Why have ye not brought him? The officers answered, NEVER MAN SPAKE LIKE THIS MAN.

    John 7:45-46

2. **You are being trained to know what to preach.**

    THE VOICE SAID, CRY. AND HE SAID, WHAT SHALL I CRY? All flesh is grass, and all the goodliness thereof is as the flower of the field: The grass withereth, the flower fadeth: because the spirit of the Lord bloweth upon it: surely the people is grass. The grass withereth, the flower fadeth: but the word of our God shall stand for ever.

    Isaiah 40:6-8

    And as ye go, preach, saying, the kingdom of heaven is at hand.

    Matthew 10:7

Many ministers preach things that they are not called to preach. Today, the pulpit is filled with people who speak on economic and financial matters. Today, pulpits are occupied by people who do not preach the word of God. The word of God is unattractive to carnal people.

41

One day I preached in someone's church and he said, "Today you have killed money in my church." This pastor was so sad because he felt my teachings on missions, sacrifice and evangelism would make people give a much lower offering. He sadly exclaimed, "You have killed the offering today." However, when I did take an offering, the people gave generously.

3. You are being trained to go somewhere.

Now the word of the LORD came unto Jonah the son of Amittai, saying, Arise, go to Nineveh, that great city, and cry against it; for their wickedness is come up before me.

Jonah 1:1-2

And the word of the Lord came unto Jonah the second time, saying, Arise, go unto Nineveh, that great city, and preach unto it the preaching that I bid thee.

Jonah 3:1-2

God wants to send you somewhere. Are you ready to go? Many people fulfil their destiny when they travel away from their home.

Now the Lord had said unto Abram, Get thee out of thy country, and from thy kindred, and from thy father's house, unto a land that I will shew thee:

Genesis 12:1

Abraham had to leave his kinsfolk and leave the country he was familiar with. God sent him away from his own family and his own country. Are you prepared to be great like father Abraham? You may have to go somewhere.

4. You are being trained to be able to live anywhere.

I know both how to be abased, and I know how to abound: every where and in all things I am instructed

both to be full and to be hungry, both to abound and to suffer need.

Philippians 4:12

Christians who are useless as far as the kingdom is concerned are those who have decided that they can only live in certain rich nations. Paul did not have to be in Rome or anywhere like that. He was instructed to abound and also to abase. That means he could live anywhere, once he needed to serve the Lord. Paul was ready to live in Rome and he was ready to live anywhere else.

CHAPTER 8

To Prepare is to Lay a Foundation

If the foundations be destroyed, what can the righteous do?

Psalm 11:3

Without foundations, the righteous cannot do much. Every man of God needs to have a solid foundation. When you have a solid foundation, you can build a solid structure. God wants you to prepare by laying a solid foundation. The foundations of God are sure foundations.

NEVERTHELESS THE FOUNDATION OF GOD STANDETH SURE, having this seal, The Lord knoweth them that are his. And, Let every one that nameth the name of Christ depart from iniquity. But in a great house there are not only vessels of gold and of silver, but also of wood and of earth; and some to honour, and some to dishonour. If a man therefore purge himself from these, he shall be a vessel unto honour, sanctified, and meet for the master's use, and prepared unto every good work. Flee also youthful lusts: but follow righteousness, faith, charity, peace, with them that call on the Lord out of a pure heart.

2 Timothy 2:19-22

You Must Lay Six Foundations for Your Ministry

There are six foundations that you must lay if you are to prepare properly for the work of God. These six foundations will ensure that you are established in ministry. These six foundations will ensure that you do not break down in the middle of your calling.

1. **Prepare for the gospel by laying the foundation of repentance.**

    Therefore leaving the principles of the doctrine of Christ, let us go on unto perfection; not laying again the FOUNDATION OF REPENTANCE from dead works, and of faith toward God, Of the doctrine of baptisms, and of laying on of hands, and of resurrection of the dead, and of eternal judgment. And this will we do, if God permit.

    Hebrews 6:1-3

45

Prepare for the ministry by laying a foundation of repentance. Repentance is turning away from sin. When you turn away from your past life, you lay a foundation for a great ministry. Every one has made mistakes! Everyone has sin and evil in his life! Without turning away completely, you will never become what God wants you to become. Repentance is the ability to turn around. Repentance is the ability to move away from the evil that you were once involved with.

Today, the foundation of repentance has been eroded in the church. People who were drug addicts continue to live with their addictions. People who were sexual perverts continue to be sexual perverts. People who were fornicating continue to live in fornication. People who were drunkards continue to live in alcoholism. Because of this, the foundation of repentance is removed.

The foundation of repentance is not about being perfect. The foundation of repentance is about the ability to turn away from sin and evil. Judas attempted to turn away from his sin. But he did not turn away completely. He just admitted that he had made a mistake to betray innocent blood. But he was not prepared to go through the process that is required when a person is repenting.

There are manifestations of repentance that every Christian needs to understand. When a person really repents, there are things that we see on the outside that help us to accept that the person has truly repented.

There must be a clearing of yourself. There must be indignation at what you have done wrong and there must be fear, desire and zeal for the right thing. There must even be revenge where you seek to undo whatever wrongs have been done.

Now I rejoice, not that ye were made sorry, but that ye sorrowed to repentance: for ye were made sorry after a godly manner, that ye might receive damage by us in nothing. For godly sorrow worketh repentance to salvation not to be repented of: but the sorrow of the world worketh death. For behold this selfsame thing, that ye sorrowed after a godly sort, what carefulness it wrought in you, yea, what clearing of yourselves, yea, what indignation, yea, what fear, yea, what vehement desire, yea, what zeal, yea, what revenge! In all things ye have approved yourselves to be clear in this matter.

2 Corinthians 7:9-11

Because people do not really repent, they do not go far from their past lives. Across the world today, you can see many Christians wallowing in the same old sins that they lived in when they were in the world. It is time to rebuild the foundations of repentance by turning away from sin, turning away from old girlfriends, turning away from old boyfriends, and turning away from old associations. These foundations are just as important today as they were yesterday. Turning away from drugs, turning away from addictions, turning away from cigarettes, turning away from all pollutions that destroy the human life is as important today as it has ever been. Make sure you lay the foundation of repentance from dead works in your life and ministry.

2. Prepare for the gospel by laying the foundation of being a man of faith.

Therefore leaving the principles of the doctrine of Christ, let us go on unto perfection; not laying again the FOUNDATION OF repentance from dead works, and of FAITH TOWARD GOD, of the doctrine of baptisms, and of laying on of hands, and of resurrection of the dead, and of eternal judgment. And this will we do, if God permit.

Hebrews 6:1-3

Faith towards God is an important foundation of the ministry. All through the Bible we see the importance of having faith. Without faith you cannot please God! (Hebrews 11:6) Without faith you cannot walk with God because we walk by faith! (2 Corinthians 5:7) Without faith you cannot live in God because the just shall live by their faith! (Hebrews 10:38)

Without faith you cannot please God. There is almost nothing you can do when you do not have faith. Rise up and become someone who listens to preaching. Listen to audio messages and watch videos. As you listen to the word of God being preached, your faith will be built up and you will be laying a great foundation for your ministry.

3. **Prepare for the gospel by laying the foundation of baptisms.**

   Therefore leaving the principles of the doctrine of Christ, let us go on unto perfection; not laying again THE FOUNDATION OF repentance from dead works, and of faith toward God, of THE DOCTRINE OF BAPTISMS, and of laying on of hands, and of resurrection of the dead, and of eternal judgment. And this will we do, if God permit.

   Hebrews 6:1-3

There are three baptisms that make up your strong foundation. The baptism into Christ, the baptism into the Holy Spirit and the baptism into a man of God.

A great foundation for your ministry will be laid when you are established in baptisms. There are three major baptisms you need for the ministry. First of all, you must be baptised into Christ. The scriptures teach us that water baptism is very important. Jesus said that, "He that believeth and is baptised will be saved" (Mark 16:16).

The second baptism that you need is the baptism into the Holy Spirit. You must be baptised into the Holy Spirit! Without being baptised in the Holy Spirit, you will not receive the power you need to overcome in this world. It is not easy to be a Christian. It is not easy to walk in the Spirit. It is not easy to stay on the narrow path. The reason why there are more people on the broad way is because it is far easier to do what the masses are doing.

Today, it is important that you turn away from the broad way and go up the narrow, hard and difficult path Jesus has chosen for us. There is a great reward at the end of it. The only way you can walk on this narrow path is to receive the Holy Spirit.

I pity Christians who do not have the foundation of being baptized in the Holy Spirit. Jesus said you shall receive power after the Holy Spirit comes upon you and you will be my witnesses.

When you receive the baptism of the Holy Spirit and start speaking in tongues, you become a witness, you become empowered, you become strengthened and you are able to walk with God and in God's will.

Beginning from today, receive the power of the Holy Spirit and be empowered to walk as a true Christian is expected to walk.

The third baptism that you must be baptised into is the baptism unto a man of God.

Moreover, brethren, I would not that ye should be ignorant, how that all our fathers were under the cloud, and all passed through the sea; AND WERE ALL BAPTIZED UNTO MOSES in the cloud and in the sea;

1 Corinthians 10:1-2

When God calls you to the ministry, you must be baptised unto the servant He is leading you to be associated with. The scripture above teaches us that the children of Israel were baptised unto Moses. Who are you being baptised unto? You must be immersed into the person's ministry. You must soak in the person's life and calling and become a copy of whoever God is calling you to be like.

It is time to enjoy the baptisms unto God's servants. Today people are ashamed to say whom they are associated with. But the children of Israel were baptised unto Moses and were not ashamed. If God has called you to be associated with someone or to be plunged into someone, do it wholeheartedly and you will see the changes that come into your life.

It is common to see pastors who have no one that they are following. Every disciple in the New Testament was following someone. If you do not follow someone, you will be lifeless and powerless. There are many ministers who are like atoms floating along and not actually connected to anything. It is time to accept that God has called you to be baptised unto His servant, just as the children of Israel were baptised unto Moses.

4. **Prepare for the gospel by laying the foundation of having hands laid on you.**

Therefore leaving the principles of the doctrine of Christ, let us go on unto perfection; not laying again THE FOUNDATION OF repentance from dead works, and of faith toward God, of the doctrine of baptisms, and of LAYING ON OF HANDS, and of resurrection of the dead, and of eternal judgment. And this will we do, if God permit.

Hebrews 6:1-3

The foundation of having hands laid on you is key to your ministry. You will become what God wants you to become because of the hands that are laid on you. We have viruses that spread by contact. The power to kill is being released by simple human contact. Thousands died from the corona virus because they encountered, touched or interacted with someone who had it. Laying on of hands or contact with hands is a foundational doctrine. Quality hands must be laid on you! The quality of your ministry depends on the quality of the hands that are laid on you!

Start counting the different hands that have been laid on you and start counting the hands you have come into contact with. It will reveal to you the kind of power and grace you are carrying. God is calling you today to lay a good foundation by having certain hands laid on you.

Do not expect to feel anything. Once the hands come in contact with your head, you are blessed. Expect and believe that something has happened to you when hands are laid on you.

There have been times when I have shaken hands with people and they fell down under the power. The transmission of power does not have to be in a church. It can be anywhere. The foundation of quality hands being laid on you will ensure that your ministry goes very high. Do not be fixated on falling down. Focus on the blessing that comes by hands being laid on you.

5. **Prepare for the gospel by laying the foundation of living for the resurrection.**

    Therefore leaving the principles of the doctrine of Christ, let us go on unto perfection; not laying again THE FOUNDATION OF repentance from dead works, and of faith toward God, of the doctrine of baptisms, and of laying on of hands, and of RESURRECTION OF THE DEAD, and of eternal judgment. And this will we do, if God permit.

    Hebrews 6:1-3

The resurrection of Jesus Christ and the new life that comes after this life is a mighty foundation of ministry. If your eyes and your heart are not fixed on the resurrection and eternal life, your ministry will veer off into vain jangling. There are many vain janglers around today. They jangle about economics. They jangle about all sorts of high-sounding topics. They seem to be sewing words together as though they are tailors or seamstresses who are seeking to join bits of cloth together.

There is no need to join English words together to make up high-sounding clichés. Just preach the word of God! Preach what Jesus preached! Teach parables! Teach the stories that Jesus taught us!

If you preach the Bible, your mind will be on the resurrection and the eternal life that comes after. An eternity-minded man of

God is very different from someone who is a social commentator or a secular businessman. True preachers of the Word are conscious of eternity and of the resurrection of Jesus Christ. Our whole lives are dependent on the fact that the resurrection of Jesus is true.

When that foundation of ministry is taken away, we have emptiness in the pulpit. Make sure that the foundation of the resurrection of Jesus Christ is on your heart all the time. When you do this, you will be laying a sure foundation for your life and ministry. This foundation will be eternity-consciousness as well as the consciousness of heaven and hell.

6. **Prepare for the gospel by laying the foundation of being conscious of eternal judgment.**

   Therefore leaving the principles of the doctrine of Christ, let us go on unto perfection; not laying again THE FOUNDATION OF repentance from dead works, and of faith toward God, of the doctrine of baptisms, and of laying on of hands, and of resurrection of the dead, and of ETERNAL JUDGMENT. And this will we do, if God permit.

   Hebrews 6:1-3

Eternal judgment is a key foundation that will keep every minister on course. In every school there are people who are conscious of the exam they are going to write at the end of the term. In every school there are many people who never think of exams till the last moment. That is exactly how people are in life. Most people's minds are not on eternal judgment.

People's minds are on the money they can get today and the cars they can get tomorrow. Those whose minds are on eternal judgment are those who have a true foundation of ministry. They are the ones whom God can use.

A man of God is someone whose mind is constantly on eternal judgment.

For we must all appear before the judgment seat of Christ; that every one may receive the things done in his body, according to that he hath done, whether it be good or bad.

2 Corinthians 5:10

If you are going to stand before the judgment seat of Christ, you must ask yourself what you will say and how you will explain yourself. How will you explain yourself before the Lord when you were so earthly-minded and never gave two winks for what would happen in eternity?

The scripture below tells us that the foundation shall be broken and great pain shall be in Ethiopia. Without foundational thoughts of eternity, you can never be in the ministry. How will you explain yourself before the Lord? You neglect His work and follow after silver and gold all the time. A man whose mind is on eternal judgment will not give himself to heap up earthly treasures.

And the sword shall come upon Egypt, and great pain shall be in Ethiopia, when the slain shall fall in Egypt, and they shall take away her multitude, AND HER FOUNDATIONS SHALL BE BROKEN DOWN.

Ezekiel 30:4

Just look around you and you will see two kinds of ministers of God. There are those who have the foundation of being conscious of eternal judgment and those who are conscious of the cars they drive, the house they have and the amount of money they have in the bank. Without foundational thoughts of eternity, you can never successfully be in the ministry.

CHAPTER 9

To Prepare is to be Furnished with Scripture

But continue thou in the things which thou hast learned and hast been assured of, knowing of whom thou hast learned them; AND THAT FROM A CHILD THOU HAST KNOWN THE HOLY SCRIPTURES, which are able to make thee wise unto salvation through faith which is in Christ Jesus. ALL SCRIPTURE IS GIVEN BY INSPIRATION OF GOD, AND IS PROFITABLE for doctrine, for reproof, for correction, for instruction in righteousness: That the man of God may be perfect, throughly furnished unto all good works.

2 Timothy 3:14-17

S cripture is what makes you ready for ministry. The ministry is all about reproving people, teaching doctrines, correcting people and giving instructions in righteousness. That is what a minister of God spends his life doing. If you do not know the scriptures, you will not be ready for the work of God. All scripture is given by inspiration of God. Scripture is profitable for doctrine and for reproving people.

1. The Holy Scriptures make you ready to give out doctrines.

Every minister of God has to deliver a body of teachings to the people. You have to be a master of the scriptures to be able to do this. A doctrine is a set of teachings that are presented by the teacher. A doctrine is a body of teaching and instruction that people rely on for their day-to-day lives. Your understanding of the scriptures will enable you to give out doctrines to people. Get ready to deliver a body of teachings and instructions to the people you are leading.

2. The Holy Scriptures make you able to reprove others.

Through the scriptures you will have the ability to rebuke people who are out of the way. Being a good pastor does not mean that you only sing the praises of people. It is birds that have only one song! Some men of God feel that you must say only nice things so that people will like you. Indeed, people will love you when you rebuke them according to the Holy Scriptures.

3. The Holy Scriptures make you correct people.

Many people are making mistakes and need to be corrected. They need to be set on the right path. People are making mistakes in their marriages. People are making mistakes in their finances. People are making mistakes in their personal lives. It is only through the Holy Scriptures that you will have something to say about all these things. A solid foundation in the Holy Scriptures is necessary if you are going to correct the people.

4. The Holy Scriptures make you able to instruct people in righteousness.

What is the right thing? As a human being, you are filled with unrighteousness yourself. You are full of error! You are full of mistakes! Who are you to instruct anyone in righteousness?

Through the word of God, you are able to open your mouth and instruct people in righteousness. People will listen to your instructions because they are not your instructions but they are instructions from the scripture.

5. The Holy Scriptures make you thoroughly furnished for every good work.

When you have the Holy Scripture you are thoroughly furnished for all good works. Because of the word of God, you will be ready to reprove, to correct and to instruct people. You will be ready to lay out doctrines and deliver a series of teachings for the people of God.

All these are made possible because you know the word of God. It is important that you become thoroughly furnished with the word of God so that you can be ready for all the good works that God is planning to use you for. There is no area of the ministry that you will not be equipped for when you know the Holy Scriptures!

6. The Holy Scriptures tell you what you should preach.

I charge thee therefore before God, and the Lord Jesus Christ, who shall judge the quick and the dead at his appearing and his kingdom; PREACH THE WORD; be instant in season, out of season; reprove, rebuke, exhort with all longsuffering and doctrine.

2 Timothy 4:1-2

Paul charges ministers to preach the Word, to stay with the Word. If you do not preach the word of God, you will deviate into vain jangling. There is no need for your empty speeches on finances and economic empowerment. Preach the Word! As soon as you lay aside the word of God you will go into error.

7. The Holy Scriptures make you approved unto God.

STUDY TO SHEW THYSELF APPROVED UNTO GOD, a workman that needeth not to be ashamed, rightly dividing the word of truth. But shun profane and vain babblings: for they will increase unto more ungodliness.

2 Timothy 2:15-16

You do not need the approval of men. Do not worry about what people think of you. Just make sure that God thinks highly of you. You will become a workman who is not ashamed!

A man of God had a vision in which he went to heaven. He met a pastor who had died some years earlier. This pastor spoke about what happened to him on his judgment day. He said when he arrived in heaven and saw the books he had written whilst on earth, he was so ashamed of them. He wanted to grind them into powder. This pastor had written books that were full of truth but were empty of the word of God. He was completely disapproved of in heaven. No one wanted to see him in heaven. No one was happy to see him in heaven. Following the Holy Scriptures is going to help you to be approved in heaven.

CHAPTER 10

To Prepare is to be Ready for War

PREPARE YE WAR AGAINST HER; arise, and let us go up at noon. Woe unto us! For the day goeth away, for the shadows of the evening are stretched out.

Jeremiah 6:4

W ar is something that you prepare for. The ministry is war! Preparing to preach the gospel is preparing for war. You are preparing to attack an enemy and you must get yourself ready. Your enemy has been fighting for years. Your enemy has fought many other people. Your enemy knows you better than you can imagine, because you are just like someone he has fought before. The enemy has prepared his defences.

He shall recount his worthies: they shall stumble in their walk; they shall make haste to the wall thereof, and THE DEFENCE SHALL BE PREPARED.

Nahum 2:5

You must also prepare your defences. Without your defences you will be easy prey for the enemy. Without your defences, the devil will make quick mincemeat of you. You need to get yourself properly armed for the battle of ministry. I remember one war in which the Germans were invading Russia. At a point in the war, the Russians were not expecting to be attacked and they were taken by surprise. Because of this, many of the Russian soldiers did not have rifles. They were asked to charge at the enemy who were properly armed with guns. Some of the Russians were able to pick up and use the guns of dead soldiers around them. Indeed, it must have been terrible to have had to charge the enemy line without any weapons. This is what God wants to protect you from.

(For the weapons of our warfare are not carnal, but mighty through God to the pulling down of strong holds;) Casting down imaginations, and every high thing that exalteth itself against the knowledge of God, and bringing into captivity every thought to the obedience of Christ;

2 Corinthians 10:4-5

It is time for you to believe in the weapons and defences God has given you. The weapons of your warfare are not what you would think they should be. They do not look like mighty weapons but they are! The armour of God does not even sound like it is a powerful defence, but that is what will protect you.

I used to think that Apostle Paul was using some kind of poetry to paint a picture of the armour of God, to teach us the importance of righteousness, faith, truth, the gospel and the word of God, etc.

Over time, I have come to realise that the weapons mentioned in the armour of God are the only defence a minister has against demonic attacks and wicked surprises. *I promise you, any attack, (no matter the type of attack) you will ever experience in the future, will be neutralized if this armour is on!* If you do not have the armour of God on, you will go down when you are attacked by the enemy. The enemy has a series of surprises waiting for you. It is impossible to tell exactly how he will come against you. You can overcome these surprises by putting on the full armour.

Put on the whole armour of God, that ye may be able to stand against the wiles of the devil. For we wrestle not against flesh and blood, but against principalities, against powers, against the rulers of the darkness of this world, against spiritual wickedness in high places. Wherefore take unto you the whole armour of God, that ye may be able to withstand in the evil day, and having done all, to stand.

Stand therefore, having your loins girt about with truth, and having on the breastplate of righteousness; And your feet shod with the preparation of the gospel of peace; Above all, taking the shield of faith, wherewith ye shall be able to quench all the fiery darts of the wicked. And take the helmet of salvation, and the sword of the Spirit, which is the word of God:

Ephesians 6:11-17

1. Prepare for war by putting on the breastplate of righteousness.

The breastplate of righteousness is one of the most important weapons. If you set aside the breastplate of righteousness, many surprise attacks of the enemy against you will succeed. All accusations against you will successfully bring you down if the breastplate of righteousness is not on.

Without the breastplate of righteousness, an attack of slander will destroy you! Without the breastplate of righteousness, an attack of gossip will affect you! But the breastplate of righteousness will protect you from the backbiting tongue. The breastplate of righteousness will protect you from the strange woman. The breastplate of righteousness will protect you from traitors.

A traitor is somebody who pretends to be on your side for a long time. A traitor is an outsider who pretends to be an insider. A traitor is looking for information that can destroy you but the breastplate of righteousness will protect you from such traitors.

2. Prepare for war by putting on the belt of truth.

The belt of truth will protect you from many evils. The devil is the father of lies. The belt of truth will protect you from having the presence of a demon in your life. The belt of truth will protect you from falsehood and deception. The belt of truth will protect you from becoming a hypocrite.

Remember that Jesus disliked hypocrites the most. A hypocrite is someone who has grown in deception until he pretends about everything. Hypocrisy and treachery are the worst evils that can befall you.

Many pastors are hypocrites because they look good on the outside but inwardly are full of evil. The belt of truth will protect you from this devastating evil that destroyed the religious Pharisees.

The belt of truth will protect you from internally growing evils. Most thieves, adulterers, fornicators are also liars. The lies protect them from being discovered. Their lies are necessary to enable them to continue in their evil ways. The belt of truth will also protect you from self-deception.

3. Prepare for war by taking the shield of faith.

The shield of faith will also protect you from many evils. The shield of faith will protect you from becoming secularized and humanistic. The shield of faith will protect you from becoming prayerless. People without faith do not pray. The shield of faith will quench the attacks of the enemy. The shield of faith will keep you walking on in God's will. Paul said, "I have kept the faith" (2 Timothy 4:7). Many ministers do not keep the faith and do not believe what they used to believe in the beginning of their ministries.

Faith will keep you walking in the centre of God's will. Without faith, you will drown in the Red Sea of your life. Without faith, you will not be able to do the impossible any more.

Indeed, you will be able to do very little without the shield of faith. Without the shield of faith, you will be paralysed by the circumstances of life. Without faith, you will no longer be able to subdue nations. Nations will rather subdue you!

You must become a great man of faith! This is one of your top defences. It is also one of your top attacking weapons.

4. Prepare for war by taking the sword of the Spirit.

The sword of the Spirit is an important weapon you need to have. Jesus defended Himself against the devil by quoting key scriptures. You need to memorize many scriptures if you want to have the sword of the Spirit. The scriptures you have memorized are your sword. The deeper your understanding of scripture, the more versatile you are with the sword. People who have thrown away the sword of the Spirit have taken up sticks and grass as weapons.

Using sticks and grass as your weapons make you look foolish in the spirit. Demons see men of God holding twigs instead of the mighty sword of the Spirit. You cannot fight the enemy with grass, weeds or twigs. You need a real sword that cuts and divides the enemy into pieces.

Many ministers have turned away from the word of God into vain jangling. Motivational speeches and comforting secular ideas to encourage the masses are not the same as the word of God. Demons have grown bolder and bolder in the church as ministers of the gospel have declined to preach the pure word of God. How happy the demons are to see a pastor who does not know his scriptures!

Those who propagate sexual perversions are happy to see priests and pastors of churches set aside the word of God and accept sin and evil into the priesthood. It is only when you set aside the sword of the Spirit that all forms of sexual perversions are accepted in the church. These practices may be acceptable in the world today but the Holy Scriptures teach against them. The church is defenceless and destroyed when it sets aside the sword of the Spirit which is the word of God.

5.   Prepare for war by putting on the helmet of salvation.

The helmet of salvation protects your head. Preaching about salvation, emphasizing salvation, offering salvation protects you from evil. It protects the church from a slow but demonic deterioration. The helmet of salvation protects the church from being destroyed and being converted into a secular institution.

Salvation is the most important topic in the Bible. God so loved the world that He gave His only begotten Son so that mankind could be saved. The purpose of God is for salvation. Numerous evils have crept into the church as salvation has been set aside. Today, people preach on every topic except salvation.

I once preached in a church and did an altar call for salvation. The bishop of the church told me, "You are the only person who did an altar call for salvation during this convention." There had been several powerful speakers. They were all ministers of the gospel but no one had spoken about salvation nor offered people a chance to be saved. As pastors have set aside the helmet of salvation, all sorts of secular unspiritual attitudes have crept into the church.

Because the helmet of salvation (the emphasis of salvation) has been set aside, the church has become a centre for those seeking financial gain and getting "divine escapes" from poverty. Greed and the grasping for material things have taken centre stage in the church. The reason for which Christ died has been set aside and there is no more blessing in the church.

6. Prepare for war by putting the gospel on your feet.

Preaching the gospel of Jesus Christ is a protection and a defence for the church. Those who have stopped preaching the gospel have opened themselves wide to the enemy. All those who do not preach the gospel end up preaching other things. Preaching the gospel turns you into an evangelist. It makes you full of the fire of God.

Look closely at a church which preaches the gospel, conducts crusades, evangelistic campaigns, conducts door to door witnessing programs, has breakfast meetings, outreach lunches, passes out tracts and does evangelism in secondary schools. This church will be devoid of certain evils. Such churches will be saved from the spirit of backsliding.

A church that has only manifestations, financial breakthroughs and prophetic conventions is quite different from one that has evangelistic gospel campaigns as well. Evangelistic gospel campaigns seem to be out of fashion in many big ministries. The absence of these gospel evangelistic campaigns is an open door for demonic attacks on the churches. Churches that seem dead today were once centres of evangelistic activity.

7. Prepare for war by taking up all prayer in the Spirit.

Praying always in the Spirit is perhaps one of the greatest defences against demonic attacks. When you pray in the Spirit, no one understands what you are saying. In the Spirit however, you speak mysteries to God. There are many things that are happening around that you have no idea about.

There are traitors, there are treacherous people who are always conniving, scheming and planning things. How will you know what is going on?

There are things that you will never know. Howbeit, in the Spirit you can combat the enemy and neutralize developing plans of satan. God will give you the upper hand against demonic surprises. Through prayer, God will give you the upper hand against spiritual serpents, spiritual lions, spiritual flies and all evil spiritual birds that are launching attacks against you.

Anyone who does not pray in the Spirit is susceptible to demonic attacks. If you look at every Christian group, you will notice there are different levels of spirituality. Over time, you will notice that the least spiritual and prayerless members of the team fall off.

They are often attacked by the devil who sees wide gaps in their armour. Remember that you are fighting an enemy who can see you but whom you cannot see. Put on the whole armour of God and do not leave out any sections!

CHAPTER 11

To Prepare is to Put into a State of Readiness

So, as much as in me is, I am ready to preach the
gospel to you that are at Rome also. For I am not
ashamed of the gospel of Christ: for it is the power of
God unto salvation to every one that believeth; to the
Jew first, and also to the Greek.

Romans 1:15-16

To prepare is to enter into a constant state of readiness.

It is important to be in a state of constant readiness for whatever God wants you to do. God is calling you and you must be ready all the time. God may need you today and not next year so you must be ready all the time.

How to be Ready

1. **Be ready in every season.**

    Preach the word; be instant in season, out of season; reprove, rebuke, exhort with all longsuffering and doctrine.

    2 Timothy 4:2

    There are people who feel that they must work for God in a particular season of their lives. People especially feel that they must work for God in the twilight of their lives. The twilight of your life is the last season of your life, just before you die.

    Who told you that God's work can wait until you are about to die? God cannot wait for you. You must wait for Him! Scripture teaches us to be ready in season and out of season. Being ready in season and out of season means being ready all the time.

2. **Be ready to receive the word quickly and act quickly.**

    AND THUS SHALL YE EAT IT; WITH YOUR LOINS GIRDED, YOUR SHOES ON YOUR FEET, AND YOUR STAFF IN YOUR HAND; AND YE SHALL EAT IT IN HASTE: it is the Lord's passover. For I will pass through the land of Egypt this night, and will smite all the firstborn in the land of Egypt, both man and beast; and against all the gods of Egypt I will execute judgment: I am the Lord.

    Exodus 12:11-12

Eating the Passover meal was done in a state of readiness. God was going to judge the gods of Egypt. The demonic powers of Egypt would be destroyed by the visitation of God's judgment. The children of God needed to move with speed to escape from evil judgment. A state of readiness is necessary to escape from the world and become a preacher of the gospel.

3. **Be ready to preach the gospel in any country. Some people only want to preach the gospel in their hometown.**

   So, as much as in me is, I AM READY TO PREACH THE GOSPEL TO YOU THAT ARE AT ROME also.

   Romans 1:15

   Paul was ready to preach the gospel in every known city. Are you ready to preach the gospel in every town or do you just want to preach the gospel in America? Why do you want to just remain in Europe? Why are you not prepared to preach the gospel in Mali, in Niger, in Bolivia, in Mongolia and in Mauritania?

4. **Be ready in your mind.**

   And not that only, but who was also chosen of the churches to travel with us with this grace, which is administered by us to the glory of the same Lord, and declaration of YOUR READY MIND:

   2 Corinthians 8:19

5. **Be ready to give. You must be ready to give to support the preaching of the gospel.** Some people are ready to give only at the end of the month when they have been paid.

   For I know the forwardness of your mind, for which I boast of you to them of Macedonia, that Achaia was ready a year ago; and your zeal hath provoked very many.

   2 Corinthians 9:2

6. Be ready to fight the devil.

And having in a readiness to revenge all disobedience, when your obedience is fulfilled.

2 Corinthians 10:6

Satan has wreaked havoc in the world. He has destroyed people's lives. He has killed and destroyed many. People are devastated to a point where they cannot rise any longer. It is time to revenge! It is time to repair! It is time to take back territories! Look at how satan destroyed your life. What can you do to revenge the wickedness that has been wrought in your life? Be ready to take on the enemy and revenge all disobedience!

7. Be ready for every good work.

Put them in mind to be subject to principalities and powers, to obey magistrates, to be ready to every good work,

Titus 3:1

You must be in a state of readiness to do anything that is a good work. Some people come into full-time ministry and only want to do certain jobs. You must be ready for every kind of work. Recently, God told me to do something that I despised. I used to think that it was only backslidden pastors who did those jobs. I was surprised when the Lord asked me to do that good work. You must be ready for every good work.

8. Be ready to witness and preach about Jesus at any time.

But sanctify the Lord God in your hearts: and be ready always to give an answer to every man that asketh you a reason of the hope that is in you with meekness and fear:

1 Peter 3:15

You come into contact with dying souls all the time. You must be ready to preach the gospel to everybody all the time.

9. Be ready to seek God at any time.

And be ready in the morning, and come up in the morning unto mount Sinai, and present thyself there to me in the top of the mount.

Exodus 34:2

Some people only want to seek the Lord during the twenty-one day fasting at the beginning of the year. You must be able to seek the Lord at any time. If you want to be ready for the gospel, you must be ready to seek God at any time.

CHAPTER 12

To Prepare is to Set Your House in Order

In those days was Hezekiah sick unto death. And the prophet Isaiah the son of Amoz came to him, and said unto him, THUS SAITH THE LORD, SET THINE HOUSE IN ORDER; FOR THOU SHALT DIE, AND NOT LIVE. Then he turned his face to the wall, and prayed unto the Lord, saying, I beseech thee, O Lord, remember now how I have walked before thee in truth and with a perfect heart, and have done that which is good in thy sight. And Hezekiah wept sore. And it came to pass, afore Isaiah was gone out into the middle court, that the word of the Lord came to him, saying, Turn again, and tell Hezekiah the captain of my people, Thus saith the Lord, the God of David thy father, I have heard thy prayer, I have seen thy tears: behold, I will heal thee: on the third day thou shalt go up unto the house of the Lord. And I will add unto thy days fifteen years; and I will deliver thee and this city out of the hand of the king of Assyria; and I will defend this city for mine own sake, and for my servant David's sake. And Isaiah said, Take a lump of figs. And they took and laid it on the boil, and he recovered.

2 Kings 20:1-7

Everyone who goes to war knows that it is possible that he may die. It is impossible to prepare properly without preparing your mind for the possibility of death. Every good soldier knows that he may not return from the battlefield. To prepare for the gospel is to become even more aware that death is real. It is time to prepare for death because it is coming to everyone.

To set your house in order is to get ready for death and eternity.

Hezekiah was told to set his house in order. Hezekiah was told to get ready for death! Hezekiah was told to get ready for eternity! Are you ready for eternity? Hezekiah is not the only one who is being told to set his house in order and get ready for eternity. We are all being given that command.

One of the ways to get yourself ready for eternity is to prepare for the gospel and preach the gospel for the rest of your life. What you did with the gospel of Jesus Christ and whether you served the Lord or not will matter so much in eternity.

To set your house in order is to make arrangements for the end of your life on this earth and the beginning of eternity.

The sins that you have committed in this life will be used in your judgment after this life. The good things you have done in this life will also be revealed in the life to come. Preparing to preach the gospel is preparing for eternity.

To prepare for the gospel is to prepare for your death. One day you will die and you will account for what you did with your life. One of the most important things you will be judged for is the souls that you have won. He that winneth souls is wise! They that turn many to righteousness shall shine like the stars forever (Daniel 12:3).

It is wise to get ready for eternity. There are many people who do not think of eternity at all.

Get ready for eternity because without eternity we will have a miserable life.

If in this life only we have hope in Christ, we are of all men most miserable.

1 Corinthians 15:19

Get ready for eternity because one day you will be outside this body and present with the Lord.

We are confident, I say, and willing rather to be absent from the body, and to be present with the Lord.

2 Corinthians 5:8

How to Set Your House in Order

1. **Set your house in order by winning souls.**

The fruit of the righteous is a tree of life; and he that winneth souls is wise.

Proverbs 11:30

2. **Set your house in order by shining as a soul winner.**

And they that be wise shall shine as the brightness of the firmament; and they that turn many to righteousness as the stars for ever and ever.

Daniel 12:3

3. **Set your house in order by serving God with all your strength.**

Whatsoever thy hand findeth to do, do it with thy might; FOR THERE IS NO WORK, NOR DEVICE, NOR KNOWLEDGE, NOR WISDOM, IN THE GRAVE, WHITHER THOU GOEST.

Ecclesiastes 9:10

4. **Set your house in order by ensuring that you depart from this world in peace.**

    And he came by the Spirit into the temple: and when the parents brought in the child Jesus, to do for him after the custom of the law, Then took he him up in his arms, and blessed God, and said, Lord, now lettest thou thy servant depart in peace, according to thy word: For mine eyes have seen thy salvation, Which thou hast prepared before the face of all people; A light to lighten the Gentiles, and the glory of thy people Israel.

    Luke 2:27-32

    You cannot depart from this world in peace if many people have not seen the salvation of God.

    When your eyes see salvation coming to many people, you will be ready to depart in peace. You will never have peace until many people have found Jesus Christ through your ministry.

5. **Set your house in order by working while it is day. When it is night you cannot work.** When you are sick you cannot work for God. When you are too old you cannot work for God. Set your house in order by doing all you can in this moment of health and strength.

    I must work the works of him that sent me, while it is day: the night cometh, when no man can work.

    John 9:4

Conclusion

Set your house in order because you will see God very soon! Before you can say, "Jack Robinson" you will be standing before the throne of God, receiving judgment for all that you have done in this world.

May the Lord help you to walk in a state of readiness and preparation for all the good works He has called you to do! I believe there are great things God has in store for you.

The mighty works and the greater works will surely come to pass. Your faith and your obedience are revealed by your ardent preparation, rehearsals, planning and self-education.

God notices every step you take to ensure that you accomplish His will. Your readiness to serve the Lord in maturity will pay off! You will be glad about the foundations that you lay today. May the Lord give you great increase and fulfilment to the many dreams and visions of your life and ministry!

To the making of many books, there is no end! Please be blessed and encouraged with these few words on how to prepare yourself to be the best preacher of the gospel of Jesus Christ.

Made in United States
Orlando, FL
20 January 2023

28860914R00043